D1409715

WITHDRAWN

The Study of Money

Paying Without Money

Tim Clifford

Rourke
Publishing LLC
Vero Beach, Florida 32964

www.rourkepublishing.com

PHOTO CREDITS: © Szymon Aponowicz: Title Page; © Jens Stolt: page 4 bottom; © Chee Choon Fat: page 4 top; © Alistair Michael Thomas: page 5; © Rob Marmion: page 7; © Armentrout: page 8, 19 top; © Jamey Ekins: page 9; © Associated Press/ Ralph Radford: page 11; © Andre Blais: page 12; © Mikael Damkier: page 13 top; © TimmyQ: page 13 bottom; © Diana Rich: page 14; © elli: page 15; © Aleksey Kondratyuk: page 16; © Associated Press/ Michel Euler: page 17; © Library of Congress: page 18; © Losevsky Pavel: page 19 bottom; © EBay: page 21 left; © CoolCaesar: page 21 right; © iofoto: page 23; © Jeremy Swinborne: page 24; © 7016366030: page 27; © Zhu Difeng: page 28; © Debbie Gerdt: page 30 top; © Rafael Ramirez Lee: page 30 middle; © Donald Gargans: page 30 bottom

Editor: Jeanne Sturm

Cover Design: Renee Brady

Page Design: Tara Raymo

Library of Congress Cataloging-in-Publication Data

Clifford, Tim, 1959-
  Paying without money / Tim Clifford.
     p. cm. -- (The study of money)
  Includes index.
  ISBN 978-1-60472-407-3
  1. Money--Juvenile literature. 2. Payment--Juvenile literature. I. Title.
  HG221.5.C58 2009
  332.1'78--dc22

                                    2008011334

Printed in the USA

IG/IG

Table of Contents

Traditional Ways to Pay

Money is a part of our everyday lives. Yet for much of human history, there was no such thing as money. If you wanted goods or services, you had to **barter** for them. In other words, you had to exchange something you had for something else you wanted. If you grew wheat, for example, you might trade some of it for corn or other products.

With the invention of coins and paper money, paying for things became much easier. For many centuries, money was the main method of payment in the world. Today, however, there are many ways to pay without money.

The Greeks and Romans used coins 2,000 years ago, and earlier. Some of the oldest coins were made as early as 600 B.C.

4

Some ways of paying became popular because they were easier than using money. Other ways developed so that people could borrow money and pay it back at a later date.

No matter what you are buying, there are many ways to pay. How you choose to pay may depend on what you are buying, where you are buying it, or how much it costs.

The Role of Banks and Credit Unions

Banks and **credit unions** are more than just places to keep your money. They offer all kinds of **financial** services.

Opening an **account** at a financial institution, such as a bank, opens the door to many types of payment. You can use the money you deposit to get a checking account or a debit card. Many other forms of payment depend on having a bank or credit union account.

Credit unions and banks are also places to borrow money. They issue credit cards. They also loan money to people to make large purchases.

Banks and credit unions offer many online services these days. By using a computer, you can **deposit** or withdraw money, pay bills, and even apply to borrow money without ever leaving your home.

No matter how you choose to pay for things, a credit union or bank is often involved in the transaction.

Checking Accounts

One of the oldest forms of payment is the check. When you open a checking account at a bank or credit union, you are given a book of checks. When you write a check, you are telling your bank to pay a certain amount of money to the person who receives it.

Checks are much safer to use than money. If money is lost or stolen, anyone can use it. With a check, only the person you write the check to, called the **payee**, can cash it.

8

There are many parts to a check.

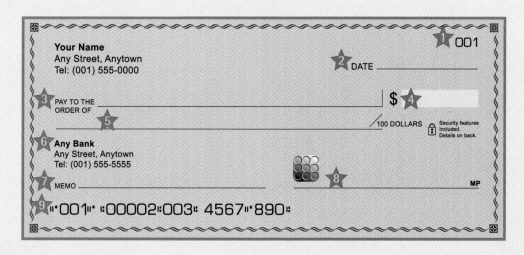

⭐ **Check Number** - *Checks are numbered so you can keep track of them.*

⭐ **Date** - *Checks may not be cashed before the date you write on them.*

⭐ **Payee** - *The payee is the person or organization to whom the check is written.*

⭐ **Amount in Numbers** - *To write a check for $35.00, you would write 35.00 on this line.*

⭐ **Amount in Words** - *To write a check for $35.00, you would write Thirty-five and 00/100 on this line.*

⭐ **Name of Financial Institution** - *This is the name of your bank or credit union.*

⭐ **Memo** - *The memo helps you remember why you wrote the check.*

⭐ **Signature** - *A check must be signed to be valid.*

⭐ **Routing number** - *Each financial institution is assigned its own number.*

Money Orders

Checks are very convenient, but they have a few drawbacks. One major drawback is that some stores and businesses don't accept them. It can also take days before a bank pays the amount written on the check.

Another problem is fraud. If blank checks are stolen, anyone can try to cash them. Also, checks can *bounce*. A check bounces when it is written for more money than is in the checking account.

One solution to these problems is to use a money order.

Money orders are like checks, but they are pre-paid. To get one, you can go to places such as banks, post offices, or convenience stores. Then you pay the amount you want to appear on the check.

There are advantages to money orders. One is that a money order can't bounce because it has already been paid for. Another is that you don't need a checking account to get a money order.

There are some disadvantages, as well. Like checks, not everyone accepts money orders. Also, you must know the total amount of your purchase in advance. Finally, it usually costs several dollars to purchase a money order. Many checking accounts are free.

Debit Cards

One extremely popular way to pay for things is by using a **debit** card. It looks very much like a credit card. It has a magnetic strip on the back that stores your checking account information. It also has your account number on the front in raised letters.

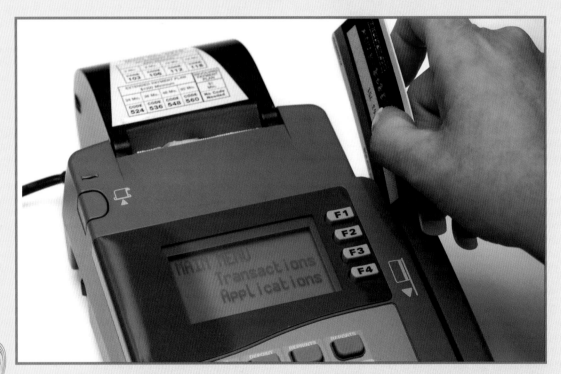

When you buy something, you swipe the card through a card reader in the store. The money is debited, or subtracted, from your checking account.

Besides shopping, people use debit cards to withdraw money from ATMs, or automatic teller machines. Debit cards are also used to make purchases over the Internet or phone.

When you get a debit card, you are assigned a PIN, or personal identification number. You must enter this pin on a keypad when you make a purchase. This helps make debit cards safe, because they can only be used if you know the PIN.

Credit Cards

Credit cards look very much like debit cards. They are the same size. Both have a magnetic strip on the back and an account number on the front. There is, however, a major difference.

When you use a credit card, you are not paying with your own money. **Credit** is an amount of money you may borrow. In other words, you are paying with money you borrow from the credit card company. This money must be paid back.

14

A great advantage of credit cards is that you can buy items that cost more money than you have. If you pay back what you borrow every month, credit cards cost little or nothing. However, if you don't pay it all back, you are charged **interest**. Interest is a **fee** paid for borrowing money. It is added to the money you owe.

Pre-paid credit cards are also available. You can purchase them at many banks and stores. You may not borrow or spend more than you paid for the card. There is no interest on pre-paid cards.

Traveler's Checks

Vacations can be expensive, and it doesn't make sense to carry a lot of cash when you travel. When you visit a country that uses a different **currency**, your cash may not be accepted. One way to solve these problems is by using traveler's checks.

You can buy traveler's checks at banks and credit unions. The amount of each check is preprinted on the front. They may be purchased in many different currencies.

It is very safe to use traveler's checks. If they are lost or stolen, they can be replaced. A refund can be given very quickly.

Traveler's checks are not as popular as they once were. Today, far more people use credit and debit cards when they travel. As a result, some vacation spots no longer accept traveler's checks.

Wire Transfers

Sending a message by telegraph is also known as *sending a wire*. Transferring money by wire is almost as old as the telegraph itself. A request to send money can be wired from one telegraph office to any other office.

Today money is often wired from bank to bank. This method is very safe, because both the sender and recipient must have an account at their banks. Because wire transfers can be expensive, they are usually used to transfer large amounts of money.

This photograph from 1908 shows a telegraph operator printing a telegram.

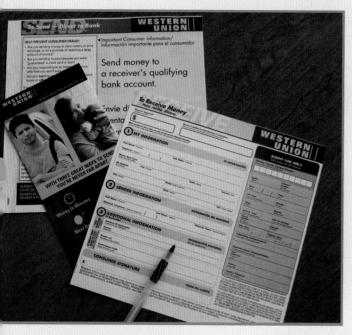

While it is usually safe to transfer money, there are some dangers. Wiring cash to pay someone you don't know is risky. They will receive the cash before you get your goods.

There are other problems with wire transfers. They can be very costly compared to other methods of payment. Also, they are not as instant as most people think. It can take hours for a transfer to occur. Even so, for sending large payments to someone far away, wire transfers are often the best choice.

19

Online Payment Services

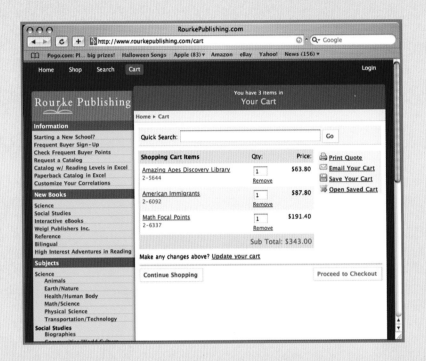

Today, it's possible to send money to people worldwide from your computer. Online payment services make this possible. Many online stores, auction sites, and other businesses accept online payments.

You must have an account with one of these services. When you pay for your online purchase, the service will automatically send the money from your checking account. This happens almost instantly. You may be charged a small fee for the transfer.

20

Meet an Important Person

Meg Whitman

In 1998, Meg Whitman became the president of eBay, the world's largest online auction site. Many of eBay's customers wanted an easy way to pay for their auction wins. They started using PayPal.com, one of the first online payment services. Before long, more than half of eBay's auctions were paid using PayPal.

In 2002, Whitman and eBay purchased PayPal for 1.5 billion dollars. Together, these two companies process millions of online payments every year.

21

Automatic Payment

If you have a lot of regular bills, it can become very time consuming to pay for them by check. Instead of licking envelopes and buying stamps, many people choose to pay for bills using automatic payments.

One way to do this is to go to the website of each company to whom you owe money and sign up. Many companies today allow for such automatic payments. The bills will be paid on the day you select. The money usually comes out of your checking account.

Many financial institutions also offer automatic payment services. To use them, you sign up with your bank or credit union. Then you specify when and how much to pay each payee.

Once it is set up, online payment services are very easy to use. The service remembers your payees and account numbers so all you have to do is enter the amount to pay. Many financial institutions offer this service for free, and there's no need to buy stamps!

Loans

Major purchases, such as a car or a boat, cost a lot of money. One way to pay for such expensive items is to take out a loan. If you qualify, a financial institution advances you the amount you need. You pay back a part of that money each month, plus interest.

One special type of loan is called a **mortgage**. This type of loan helps you afford to purchase a home. Because these loans are very large, they usually take fifteen to thirty years to pay off completely.

People who own their own homes may qualify for another type of loan called a home equity loan. **Equity** is the value of your home minus the amount of your mortgage. You can borrow against your equity to pay off bills. You pay back the money you borrow with interest.

Usually, the interest on home equity loans is far less than what credit cards charge. This can help save money when you need to borrow to pay off bills.

Value of Home $300,000
- Amount of Mortgage   *-$200,000*
= Equity   *$100,000*

Home equity loans are often used for building a swimming pool or remodeling the kitchen.

25

Identity Theft

Paying without money is very common today. To pay without money, however, you often have to give a lot of information. You must give your name, address, telephone number, credit card numbers, and more, each time you make a payment without money.

This can lead to identity theft. Identity theft occurs when someone takes your personal information and pretends to be you. They can then open bank accounts, apply for credit cards, or make purchases in your name.

Identity theft is a very common crime. Millions of people have their identities stolen every year. Once it is stolen, it is hard to get back.

The lock symbol tells you the site is secure.

To protect yourself, never give personal information to anyone you don't know or don't trust. Buy items only from known online stores or use a payment service you trust.

When paying online, make sure the web address starts with *https* (not just *http*). The extra *s* means the site is secure. Also, look for a symbol, such as a lock, on your browser. This tells you the site is secure, and not a fake site set up to steal your information.

New Payment Methods

New ways to pay without money are being developed all the time.

Paying by Cell Phone

Many people carry their cell phones everywhere they go. Why not use them to make payments? Some companies now let you pay for items by sending a message from your phone. You can even transmit a wireless signal to pay.

Paying by Precious Metal

A few online services let you buy actual gold or silver online. Paying with gold or silver coins has existed for thousands of years. Now you can simply transfer currency backed by precious metals, all on your computer.

Online Checkouts

A number of companies have started online checkout services. You can use these services to pay for goods online without having to give out your personal information.

Bartering

One of the oldest forms of payment, bartering, is suddenly new again. Using the Internet, you can exchange items you no longer need for the ones you want.

Looking to the Future

For methods of payment to catch on, they have to be easy for people to use.

Gift cards are a convenient way to pay for items in stores. Some new credit cards allow you to pay by 'waving' the card in front of a cash register. You can pay for tolls on bridges with a sticker on your car window that is read by a machine as you pass by—all without stopping your car!

With all these ways to pay, is there a need for money anymore? Will we pay for everything electronically some day? It's hard to say, but one thing is for sure. Paying without money in the future will be easier than ever before.

30

Glossary

account (uh-KOUNT): an arrangement to keep money in a bank, as in a checking account

barter (BAR-tur): to trade by exchanging food or other goods or services

credit (KRED-it): an amount of money against which you may borrow

credit unions (KRED-it YOON-yuhns): financial institutions that offers services such as savings accounts, checking accounts, and loans to their members

currency (KUR-uhn-see): the form of money used in a country

debit (DEB-it): an amount of money subtracted from a bank account

deposit (di-POZ-it): to place money in a bank account

equity (EK-wi-tee): the value of a home minus the mortgage

fee (fee): the amount of money someone charges for a service

financial (fye-NAN-shuhl): having to do with money

interest (IN-tur-ist): a fee paid for borrowing money

mortgage (MOR-gij): a loan from a bank to buy a house

payee (pay-EE): the person or organization to whom a check is written

Index

Further Reading

Allman, Barbara. *Banking*. Lerner Publications, 2005.

Bochner, Arthur, and Rose. *The New Totally Awesome Money Book for Kids*. Newmarket, 2007.

Harman, Hollis Paige. *Money Sense for Kids*. Barron's Educational Series, 2005.

Websites

www.brainpop.com/socialstudies/economics/money/
www.pbskids.org/itsmylife/money/managing/article8.html
www.kidsbank.com/

About the Author

Tim Clifford is an educational writer and the author of many nonfiction children's books. He has two wonderful daughters and two energetic Border Collies that he adopted from a shelter. Tim became a vegetarian because of his love for animals. He is also a computer nut and a sports fanatic. He lives and works in New York City as a public school teacher.